W9-CKH-125

Fog, Mist, or Haze?

by Ellen Lawrence

Consultant:

Ann M. Dillner, PhD
Associate Research Engineer
Interagency Monitoring of Protected Visual Environments (IMPROVE) Program
University of California
Davis, California

BEARPORT
PUBLISHING

New York, New York

Credits

Cover, © Cultura Creative/Alamy; TOC, © Mayovskyy Andrew/Shutterstock; 4–5, © Nature Picture Library/Alamy; 6, © Geraldas Galinauskas/Shutterstock; 7T, © MarclSchauer/Shutterstock; 7, © Radoslaw Lecyk/Shutterstock; 8T, © Mad Dog/Shutterstock; 8B, © Seqoya/Shutterstock; 9, © Richard Du Toit/Minden Pictures/FLPA; 10–11, © Mayovskyy Andrew/Shutterstock; 12T, © holbox/Shutterstock; 12B, © Chayut Thanapochoochoung/Shutterstock; 13, © Brum/Shutterstock; 13R, © Vitalii Bashkatov/Shutterstock; 14, © Creative Travel Projects/FLPA; 15, © fotokostic/istockphoto; 16, © Andrew Babble/Shutterstock; 17, © Hung Chung Chih/Shutterstock; 18T, © Ranglen/Shutterstock; 18B, © Verkhovynets Taras/Shutterstock; 19, © A Lesik/Shutterstock; 20, © Spotmatik Ltd/Shutterstock; 21, © Hung Chung Chih/Shutterstock; 22T, © Andrey Arkusha/Shutterstock; 22B, © lolostock/istockphoto; 23TL, © TTstudio/Shutterstock; 23TC, © Richard DuToit/Minden Pictures/FLPA; 23TR, © Ranglen/Shutterstock; 23BL, © Ansis Klucis/Shutterstock; 23BC, © Hung Chung Chih/Shutterstock; 23BR, © Lise Gagne/iStock.

Publisher: Kenn Goin
Senior Editor: Joyce Tavolacci
Creative Director: Spencer Brinker
Design: Emma Randall
Photo Researcher: Ruby Tuesday Books Ltd.

Library of Congress Cataloging-in-Publication Data

Lawrence, Ellen, 1967- author.
  Fog, mist, or haze? / by Ellen Lawrence.
      pages cm. — (Weather wise)
  Audience: Ages 4–9.
  Includes bibliographical references and index.
  ISBN 978-1-62724-864-8 (library binding) — ISBN 1-62724-864-1 (library binding)
  1. Water vapor, Atmospheric—Juvenile literature. 2. Fog—Juvenile literature. 3. Air—Pollution—Juvenile literature. I. Title. II. Series: Lawrence, Ellen, 1967- Weather wise.
  QC915.L39 2016
  551.57'5—dc23
                              2015011930

For more information, write to Bearport Publishing Company, Inc., 45 West 21st Street, Suite 3B, New York, New York 10010. Printed in the United States of America.

10 9 8 7 6 5 4 3 2 1

Contents

A Hidden City

It's early morning, and the sun is rising over San Francisco, California.

It's not easy to see the city and its many buildings, though.

That's because the air is filled with something thick and white.

What is this substance that's making it so difficult to see?

Is it fog, mist, or haze?

Fog, mist, and haze all float in the air. They affect how far we can see.

Covered by Fog

The thick, white substance covering San Francisco is fog.

Fog makes it hard for people to see very far.

Drivers may struggle to see other vehicles on a highway.

People might have trouble seeing each other on a sidewalk.

Even though fog is very thick, it's still light enough to float in the air.

So what is fog made of?

When you walk through fog, it feels cold and wet. Why do you think this is?

The Golden Gate Bridge in San Francisco is often hidden by fog. The bridge has special foghorns that make loud booming noises. The noises tell people on ships where the bridge is so they don't crash into it.

The Golden Gate Bridge on a clear day

The Golden Gate Bridge partially hidden by fog

What Is Fog Made Of?

Fog is made up of billions of tiny, floating water droplets.

The water may have come from the ocean, a lake, or a puddle.

So how does the water get into the air?

When the sun's heat warms up a body of water, the water changes.

Some of it turns into a **gas** called **water vapor**.

The invisible vapor then floats up into the air.

water droplets

fog

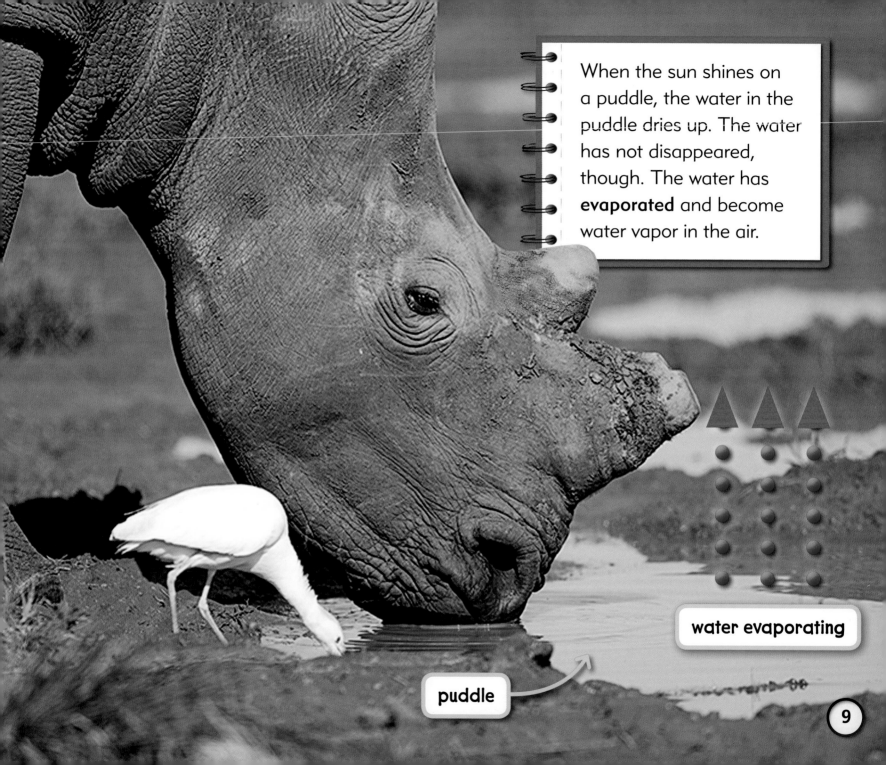

When the sun shines on a puddle, the water in the puddle dries up. The water has not disappeared, though. The water has **evaporated** and become water vapor in the air.

water evaporating

puddle

Making Fog

Once the water vapor is in the air, it can change again.

This happens when the air moves over cold ground.

The water vapor in the air cools down.

As it cools, the vapor turns into droplets of liquid water.

Then lots of tiny water droplets float in the air near the ground to make fog.

fog

Look at the fog in this picture.
It looks white and fluffy.
What does it remind you of?

The droplets of water that make up fog are too small to see. About 100 drops could fit on the period at the end of this sentence.

11

A Cloud on the Ground

Water vapor doesn't only change into water droplets close to the ground.

This change also happens high above Earth.

When water droplets collect in the sky, they are called clouds.

Clouds and fog are the same thing.

The only difference is that fog forms near the ground and clouds form in the sky!

clouds

If you've ever walked through fog—you've walked through a cloud!

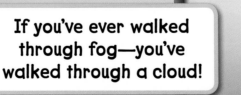

Sometimes, when it's very cold out, the tiny water droplets in fog become super cold. If they touch a tree or building, they instantly turn to ice. This type of fog is called freezing fog.

freezing fog

ice on leaves

What Is Mist?

Fog isn't the only type of cloud that forms near the ground.

Have you ever seen mist floating above a field or pond?

Just like fog, mist is made up of tiny droplets of water.

Mist is not as thick as fog, though, so it's easier to see through.

Fog and mist often disappear after a few hours. Why do you think this happens?
(See answer on page 24.)

mist above a pond

How can you tell if it's foggy or misty out? Weather scientists say that if you can see something that's about 3,300 feet (1,005 m)—or about the length of 10 football fields—away, then it's only misty. If you cannot see that far, then it's foggy.

mist

What Is Haze?

Sometimes, there is no fog or mist in the air, but it's still difficult to see very far.

It might look as if there are brownish-yellow clouds hanging in the sky.

These clouds are called haze.

Unlike fog and mist, haze is not made of water.

Haze is made of droplets of **chemicals**, solid **particles** of dust, and other **pollution**.

haze in a city

One way that pollution gets into the air is from cars and other vehicles. Most vehicles release harmful gases in their exhaust, including tiny droplets of chemicals.

haze above a highway

How else do you think pollution gets into the air?

Harmful Haze

The pollution that makes up haze gets into the air in many different ways.

Power plants and other factories release particles and gases.

Construction sites create lots of dust.

Wildfires, barbecue grills, and even indoor fireplaces make smoke and ash.

All of this pollution floats in the air.

The wind can then blow it across hundreds of miles.

In what ways are fog, mist, and haze alike? How are they different?

a power plant releasing particles and gases

a construction site producing dust

smoke from a wildfire

Haze doesn't only make it difficult for people to see. It can also make them ill. Pollution in the air, such as smoke, can hurt people's eyes and make it hard to breathe.

Clean and Clear Air

Fog, mist, and haze all make it difficult to see.

Yet they are not the same.

Fog and mist happen naturally and are not harmful for people to breathe.

Haze, however, is made from harmful pollution that people help to create.

One way that people can make less pollution is by taking fewer car trips or by walking or bicycling.

We can all help keep the air free from harmful haze!

To reduce air pollution, try carpooling with your friends.

Sometimes the air in a city is filled with thick gray or yellow smog. This happens when certain substances mix together. The word *smog* is made up from the names of two of those substances. What do you think they are?

(See answer on page 24.)

smog over the city of Shanghai, China

Science Lab

How to Make Mist

It's possible to make mist with your own breath.

Stand outdoors on a very cold day.

Take a deep breath, then slowly breathe out.

What do you see in the air?

What do you think has happened to your breath?

In a notebook, write down everything you observed. Try to use these words in your explanation.

mist   water droplets

cooled   water vapor

You can also try this experiment by breathing slowly into a freezer.

(See answers on page 24.)

Science Words

chemicals (KEM-uh-kuhlz) natural or human-made substances that can sometimes harm living things

evaporated (i-VAP-uh-*rayt*-id) changed from liquid water into water vapor

gas (GASS) matter that floats in air and is neither a liquid nor a solid; most gases, such as water vapor, are invisible

particles (PAR-tuh-kuhlz) tiny pieces of solid matter, such as dust and ash or tiny liquid drops of water or chemicals

pollution (puh-LOO-shuhn) materials, such as trash, chemicals, gases, and dust, that can damage the air, water, or soil

water vapor (WAW-tur VAY-pur) water that has changed into a gas; water vapor rises and spreads through the air

Index

Read More

Frost, Helen. *Fog (Pebble)*. North Mankato, MN: Capstone (2004).

Lawrence, Ellen. *Dirty Air (Green World, Clean World)*. New York: Bearport (2014).

Spilsbury, Louise. *What is Weather? (Let's Find Out! Earth Science)*. New York: Rosen (2014).

Learn More Online

To learn more about fog, mist, and haze, visit **www.bearportpublishing.com/WeatherWise**

About the Author

Ellen Lawrence lives in the United Kingdom. Her favorite books to write are those about animals and nature. In fact, the first book Ellen bought for herself, when she was six years old, was the story of a gorilla named Patty Cake that was born in New York's Central Park Zoo.

Answers

Page 14: Fog and mist usually disappear because the tiny water droplets dry up, or evaporate, in the sun's heat. Then they become invisible water vapor floating in the air.

Page 21: Smog is made from *smoke* and other pollution mixed with *fog*. Smog makes it very difficult to see and breathe. If people breathe in smog, it can make them sick.

Page 22: Your breath makes a small cloud of mist in the air. This happens because your warm breath contains invisible water vapor. When your breath mixed with the cold air, however, the water vapor cooled and became tiny water droplets. The cloud you made with your breath formed in the same way as mist and fog.